ACTION FIGURES

PAINTINGS OF FUN, DARING, AND ADVENTURE

BY **BOB** RACZKA

Do you like **ACTION** AND **ADVENTURE**? ARTISTS DO, BECAUSE ACTION AND ADVENTURE MAKE FOR SOME PRETTY INTERESTING ART. TAKE THE PAINTINGS IN THIS BOOK. THEY'RE FULL OF ATHLETES, ADVENTURERS, DAREDEVILS, HEROES, AND FUN LOVERS. IN OTHER WORDS, **ACTION FIGURES**. SO, DO YOU WANT TO SEE SOME FIGURES IN ACTION? TURN THE PAGE.

M MILLBROOK PRESS

Saint George and the Dragon, Paolo Uccello, ca. 1470,
National Gallery, London, England

DRAGON SLAYERS

BASEBALL PLAYERS

Baseball at Night, Morris Kantor, 1934,
Smithsonian American Art Museum, Washington, D.C.

BIG TOP
Swingers

Miss La La at the Cirque Fernando, Edgar Degas, 1879,
National Gallery, London, England

STONE
Slingers

David with the Head of Goliath,
Andrea del Castagno, ca. 1450–1455,
National Gallery of Art, Washington, D.C.

PRIZEFIGHTERS

Dempsey and Firpo,
George Bellows, 1924,
Whitney Museum of
American Art, New York

Horseback
RIDERS

Lute Strummers

Jester with a Lute, Frans Hals, 1624–1626,
Musée du Louvre, Paris, France

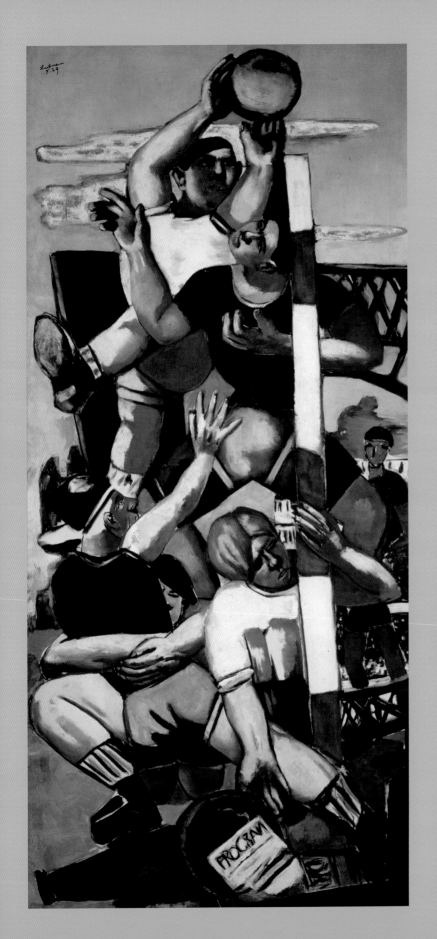

Rugby
SCRUMMERS

Rugby Players,
Max Beckmann, 1929,
Wilhelm Lehmbruck Museum,
Duisburg, Germany

Equestrienne (At the Cirque Fernando),
Henri de Toulouse-Lautrec, 1887–1888,
Art Institute of Chicago, Illinois

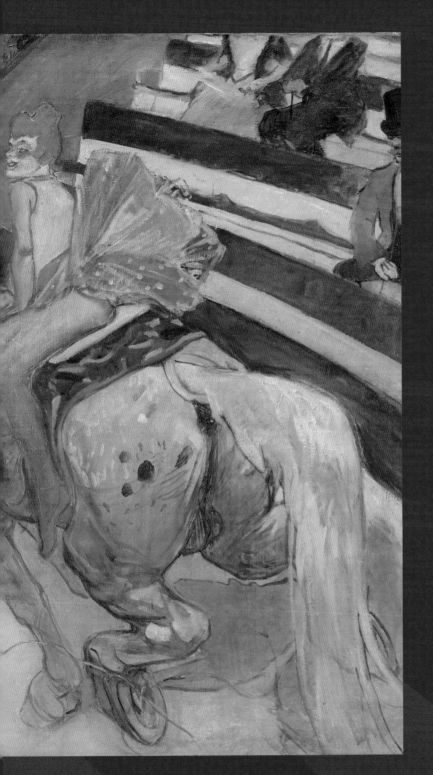

Ringmasters

Cannon Blasters

The Conquest of Mexico, Diego Rivera, 1929–1935,
Palacio Nacional, Mexico City, Mexico

High-Rise Erectors

The Construction Workers, Fernand Léger, 1950,
Musée National Fernand Léger, Biot, France

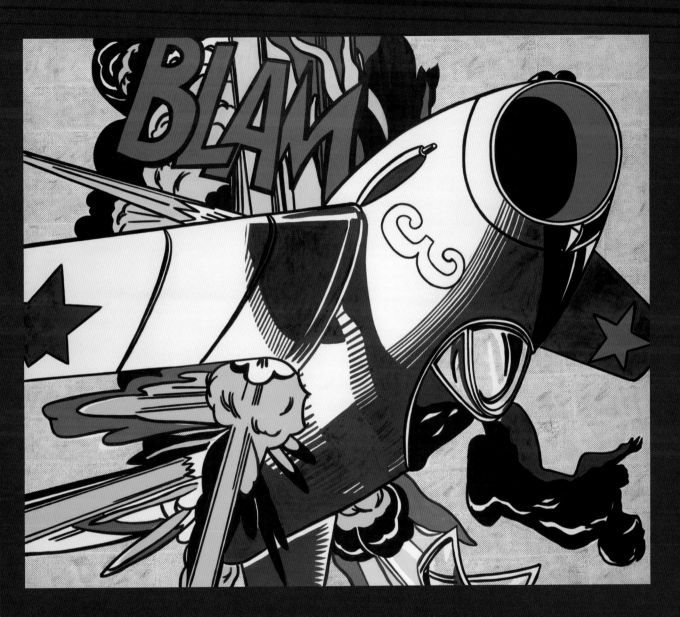

JET PLANE EJECTORS

Blam, Roy Lichtenstein, 1962,
Yale University Art Gallery, New Haven, Connecticut

The Stampede, Frederic Remington, 1908,
Gilcrease Museum, Tulsa, Oklahoma

Fredric Remington

Cattle
Drivers

Shark Bite
SURVIVORS

Watson and the Shark,
John Singleton Copley, 1778,
National Gallery of Art,
Washington, D.C.

Bicycle Racers

At the Cycle-Race Track,
Jean Metzinger, 1912,
Peggy Guggenheim Collection, Venice, Italy

Firefly Chasers

Catching Fireflies, Eishosai Choki, 1795,
The British Museum, Department of Oriental Antiquities,
London, England

Tiger Tamers

A Scene from the *Legend of Gazi*,
Unknown, ca. 1800,
The British Museum, London, England

Children's Games, Pieter Bruegel the Elder, 1560,
Kunsthistorisches Museum, Vienna, Austria

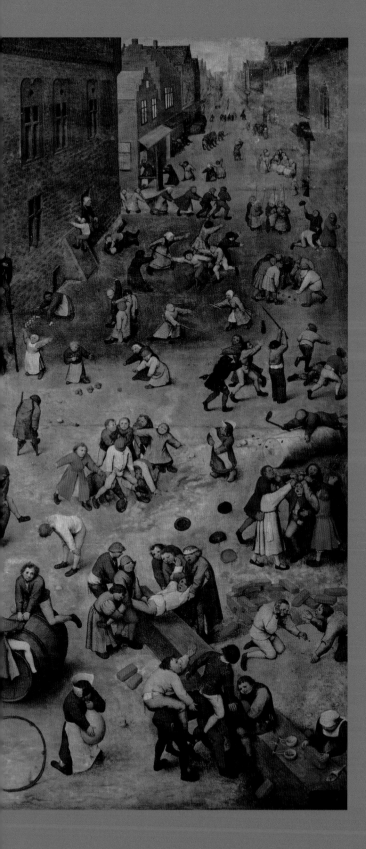

Fun and Gamers

Fun Facts about the Paintings

SAINT GEORGE AND THE DRAGON

In one story from *The Golden Legend*, a book written in the 1200s, a dragon terrorizes a city. In this scene from the story, Italian painter Paolo Uccello shows Saint George riding to the rescue on a white horse just as the princess is about to be sacrificed. Dressed in armor, George slays the dragon with his lance and saves the day.

BASEBALL AT NIGHT

The runners on first and third take their leads. The pitcher winds up. And the batter waits. U.S. artist Morris Kantor, who was born in Russia, captures the excitement of a small-town ball game, one of the first ever played at night. The first major-league night game wasn't played until the following year, in 1935.

MISS LA LA AT THE CIRQUE FERNANDO

French artist Edgar Degas loved to paint people in action. Here he shows us an acrobat named Miss La La. She is hanging by her teeth from a rope near the ceiling of the Cirque Fernando, a famous circus in Paris, France. By painting Miss La La from below and by putting her at the top of the painting with space below her, Degas makes us feel as if we are part of the audience.

DAVID WITH THE HEAD OF GOLIATH

In the biblical story of David and Goliath, the boy, David, kills the giant, Goliath, with nothing but a sling and a single stone. On this decorative shield, Italian painter Andrea del Castagno shows us both the action and its result. We see David holding the loaded sling, and we see Goliath's head at David's feet, the stone embedded in his forehead.

DEMPSEY AND FIRPO

U.S. artist George Bellows loved to paint boxers. Here, he captures one of the most famous moments in boxing history. A fighter from Argentina, Luis Firpo, knocked the heavyweight champion, Jack Dempsey of the United States, out of the ring with one punch. Surprisingly, Dempsey came back and won the fight.

LYRICAL

With just a few colorful brushstrokes, Russian painter Wassily Kandinsky makes us feel the thrill of riding a speeding horse. Kandinsky often compared painting to music. He wanted to make art that expresses our inner feelings, like music does. This painting's title, *Lyrical*, means "to have a musical quality," like a song.

JESTER WITH A LUTE

Frans Hals was a Dutch portrait painter who often captured people in the middle of an action, so they didn't look as if they were posing. In this painting, he catches the young musician looking sideways at somebody with a sly smile as he strums away on his lute, a stringed instrument like a guitar. Hals's quick, loose brushstrokes add to the feeling of movement.

RUGBY PLAYERS

Rugby is a sport similar to football. In this action-packed scene from a rugby match, German artist Max Beckmann has crammed several players into a tall, thin rectangle. Piled on top of one another, arms and legs tangled together, they all fight for the ball in a rugby play called a scrum. It feels as if the players will spill out of the canvas at any moment.

EQUESTRIENNE (AT THE CIRQUE FERNANDO)

At the same circus where Edgar Degas painted Miss La La, the acrobat, French artist Henri de Toulouse-Lautrec painted this female horseback-riding act. The brave women would dance and turn somersaults on the bare backs of the horses, while a ringmaster used a whip to keep the animals under control. This scene is a good example of Toulouse-Lautrec's sketchy, spontaneous style.

THE CONQUEST OF MEXICO

This is one part of a long three-part mural painted by Mexican artist Diego Rivera at Mexico City's National Palace, where the president's offices are. The mural shows one thousand years of Mexican history. In this sad section, we see the soldiers of Spanish conquistador Hernán Cortés firing cannons at the native Aztec people and using them as slaves.

THE CONSTRUCTION WORKERS

Because he was trained as an architect, French artist Fernand Léger was fascinated with buildings and machinery. The crisscrossing girders of this building, painted in red and yellow against a blue sky, seem to be as alive as the muscled construction workers, who are as busy as monkeys in this jungle of steel.

BLAM

U.S. artist Roy Lichtenstein found this scene of an exploding jet plane in a comic book called *All American Men of War*. Lichtenstein was famous for painting large comic-book images like this. It all started when one of his sons showed him a Mickey Mouse cartoon and said, "I bet you can't paint as good as that."

THE STAMPEDE

As a boy, U.S. artist Frederic Remington liked to draw horses and battle scenes. When he grew up, he became famous as a painter and sculptor of the American Wild West. This painting of a stampede is an exciting scene, complete with driving rain and a bolt of lightning. It shows us why he is one of the United States' best-loved artists.

WATSON AND THE SHARK

Fourteen-year-old Brook Watson, a crew member on a trading ship, was attacked by a shark while swimming. Although his heroic shipmates saved his life, he lost his right leg below the knee. Watson later became friends with U.S. painter John Singleton Copley. He may have even asked Copley to paint this scene.

AT THE CYCLE-RACE TRACK

French painter Jean Metzinger combined two art styles, Futurism and Cubism, to create this painting of a racing cyclist. By focusing on the speed and motion of the cyclist, he borrowed from the style called Futurism. By using cut-paper collage and by allowing us to "see through" parts of the cyclist, he borrowed from the style called Cubism.

CATCHING FIREFLIES

Eishosai Choki was a Japanese painter and designer of woodblock prints. In this print, he shows us a boy trying to catch fireflies, while a woman who may be his mother watches. She holds a small box to put the captured bugs in. Because this print is very old, we can see white creases, which look like tiny lightning flashes in the black sky.

A SCENE FROM THE *LEGEND OF GAZI*

Gazi Pir is a Muslim saint who lived in Bengal, a region in modern-day India and Bangledesh. It is said that he could tame wild animals. His legend is often told with the help of painted scrolls made up of twenty-seven panels. The panel in the center always shows Gazi riding a fearsome Bengal tiger. In this scroll, the unknown painter shows him holding a poisonous snake as well.

CHILDREN'S GAMES

More than four hundred years ago, the Flemish artist Pieter Bruegel the Elder painted this street scene full of fun. It shows nearly 250 children playing more than eighty games. Can you find the children playing the following twelve games?

1. Balancing a broomstick
2. Blowing soap bubbles
3. Climbing a tree
4. Doing headstands
5. Leapfrogging
6. Riding a toy horse
7. Riding piggyback
8. Rolling hoops
9. Spinning tops
10. Swimming
11. Walking on stilts
12. Wearing a mask

To Anders, a real live man of action

Text copyright © 2010 by Bob Raczka

Millbrook Press
A division of Lerner Publishing Group, Inc.
241 First Avenue North
Minneapolis, MN 55401 U.S.A.

Website address: www.lernerbooks.com

Library of Congress Cataloging-in-Publication Data

Raczka, Bob.
   Action figures : paintings of fun, daring, and adventure / by Bob Raczka.
     p.   cm.
   ISBN: 978-0-7613-4140-6 (lib. bdg. : alk. paper)
   1. Human figure in art—Juvenile literature. 2. Movement, Aesthetics of—Juvenile literature.
3. Action in art—Juvenile literature. I. Title.
   N7625.5.R33 2010
   704.9'42—dc22   2008053976

Manufactured in the United States of America
2 - DP - 3/31/10